The Plus 4 Super Sports is now one of the most sought-after models. This beautiful example is in the United States and has won many competition prizes. It is the perfect picture of power and elegance.

THE MORGAN

Ken Hill

Shire Publications Ltd

CONTENTS

Published by Shire Publications Ltd, Midland House, West Way, Botley, Oxford OX2 0PH, UK. Copyright © 1996 by Ken Hill. First published 1996; reprinted 2007. Transferred to digital print on demand 2011. Shire Library 327. ISBN 978 0 74780 328 7.

Ken Hill is hereby identified as the author of this work in accordance with Section 77 of the Copyright, Designs and Patents Act 1988.
All rights reserved. No part of this publication may be reproduced or transmitted in any form or by any means, electronic or mechanical, including photocopy, recording, or any information storage and retrieval system, without permission in writing from the publishers.

Printed in Great Britain by PrintOnDemand-Worldwide.com, Peterborough, UK.

British Library Cataloguing in Publication Data: Hill, Ken, 1933-. The Morgan. – (Shire album; no. 327). 1. Morgan automobile. I. Title. 629.2'222. ISBN-10 0-7478-0328-5. ISBN-13 978 0 74780 328 7.

Editorial Consultant: Michael E. Ware, former Curator of the National Motor Museum, Beaulieu.

ACKNOWLEDGEMENTS
The photographs on pages 1, 4, 18 (top), 19 (bottom) and 29 (top) are by John H. Sheally II. All other illustrations are from the author's collection.

Cover: *A 1956 model +4, with the original TR2 engine. (Photograph courtesy of Joe Fenstermaker)*

The SLR (Sprinzel Lawrence Racing) Plus 4 based car was designed by Chris Lawrence in conjunction with John Sprinzel. The aerodynamically shaped car is one of the three Morgans created especially for marque racing. One other car was built based on a Triumph. When it appeared in 1966 it created controversy, amongst competitors and organisers alike. The SLR Morgan achieved some notable competition successes.

Henry Frederick Stanley Morgan, known as HFS (1881-1959), founder of the Morgan Motor Company Ltd.

THE MORGAN MOTOR COMPANY

When in 1909, at the age of twenty-eight, Henry Frederick Stanley Morgan (HFS as he came to be known throughout the motoring world) designed and built his first single-seater three-wheeled experimental car, he could never have dreamt that he would become one of the world's major manufacturers of three-wheeler motor cars.

In 1901 HFS had purchased an Eagle Tandem 8 horsepower three-wheeler, which was fitted with a motorcycle-type rear wheel and conventional car-type front axle. There was a padded seat for the passenger between the front wheels (or 'closest to the accident', according to one motoring magazine). The Eagle aroused his interest in improving and developing

the design of the three-wheeled car. Three- and four-wheeled cars, particularly in the light-car and cyclecar range, had developed side by side and in about equal numbers and HFS became certain that he could improve on existing designs.

The son of a country clergyman, HFS was lucky not to be forced to enter the church as a profession. Far from discouraging him from making his own way in life, his parents and grandparents gave him every assistance. He was educated at Stone House, Broadstairs, and Marlborough College and then entered Crystal Palace Engineering College in south London, and it was here that his design and artistic talents developed. He worked as a

3

draughtsman for the Great Western Railway until 1906, when he left and went into partnership with a close friend. They opened a garage in Malvern, Worcestershire, and a few months later another in Fore Street, Worcester. The venture flourished and HFS was then able to turn his thoughts to making a car of his own design, a vehicle which would be a cross between a motorcycle and a car – not a motorcycle combination but a cyclecar.

The prototype, completed in 1909, was a single-seater fitted with tiller steering. It also incorporated Morgan's special form of sliding-pillar independent front suspension. With the addition of such refinements as rebound springs and shock absorbers, this form of front suspension is still used on the modern four-wheeler Morgan, with the exception of the Aero 8, which is fitted with a race-proved all-independent double wishbone and coil springs suspension: HFS was one of those very rare inventors who got the design right first time. The whole car was very light and was powered by a 7 horsepower Peugeot motorcycle engine. The power to weight ratio gave the vehicle a remarkable performance, a combination that has been the hallmark of the Morgan ever since.

By November 1910 the Morgan Motor Company had been formed and the partners exhibited two different models, both single-seaters, at the Motor Cycle Show at Olympia, attracting much attention but few orders. Both men were disappointed and HFS's partner decided that the business was too risky and withdrew. HFS continued alone, building a few cars to fulfil the orders that were received. He realised that, if he were to stay in business, the car had to prove itself in competitions and he must design a two-seater model. His single-seater, while suitable for his own purposes and in competition, was not a commercial proposition.

Potential customers were not particularly concerned with the design of the car. They wanted proven acceleration and speed, reliability and economy, and they looked to the various forms of motor sport to show them how various models performed. Therefore manufacturers had to be successful in racing and reliability trials if they wanted to sell cars. On Boxing Day 1910 HFS entered the first London-Exeter Two Day Trial in a JAP-engined single-seater fitted with tiller steering. He won a gold medal and received favourable press coverage. So well did his cars do in competition that at the Motor Cycle Show in November 1911 he was inundated with enquiries and orders. He realised that to maintain momentum he must enter as many sporting events as he could.

The Morgan factory at Malvern Link, Worcestershire.

4

Above: *The twin-cylinder model displayed at the 1910 Olympia Motor Cycle Show had an 8 horsepower engine and tiller steering. A conventional steering wheel was offered for an extra charge.*

Right: *This 1910 cartoon depicts the great interest shown in Morgan's single-cylinder prototype at the Olympia Motor Cycle Show.*

THE MORGAN RUNABOUT HAS A FASCINATION FOR EVERY KIND OF ROAD-USER.

As a result of the general comments received both at the 1910 show and from his friends, HFS constructed a two-seater prototype. Considerable modifications were made to it before the 1911 show.

In 1912 the company became the Morgan Motor Company Ltd and made a small but significant profit of £1314, and HFS married Ruth Day, the daughter of a local vicar. She proved to be an added driving force behind HFS, giving advice and encouragement whenever necessary. Particularly in the early years, she accompanied him on many trials and competitions, acting as 'bouncer' on the steep hills. They had five children, four girls and one boy, Peter, who eventually took over the company.

The chairman of the Morgan Motor Company Ltd was HFS's father, Prebendary H. George Morgan. In his long coat and top hat, he became a familiar figure at Brooklands and at many other events where his son was competing or attempting to break records. An extrovert, completely dedicated to the company, he would sometimes write a controversial letter to the motoring press, under a pseudonym, so as to stimulate public interest in the marque. If there was little response, he would answer himself, under a differ-

Ruth Morgan was HFS's passenger in trials. Here, at Brooklands during the 1921 Auto Cycle Union Six Day Trial, she stands behind her husband. On the left is E. B. Ware, chief experimental engineer of JAP engines.

The paint shop at the Morgan factory, Pickersleigh Road, Malvern Link, in 1929-30. The mottled dashboard of the Family model in the foreground was introduced in 1929. On the left, halfway down the workshop, is a 'Delivery' van.

ent pseudonym, in a manner likely to stimulate debate.

After his father's death in 1936 HFS became chairman and George Goodall replaced HFS as managing director, relieving him of much of the day-to-day pressure.

Continuing success in competition ensured that both sales figures and profits soared. Almost a thousand cars were sold in the year immediately before the First World War and these included exports to France, Russia, India and North and South America. In the next year a major part of the company's production had to be made over to producing shells and other munitions for the war effort. Government contracts were on a fixed profit allowance and generous by any standards, and there was financial help with the cost of new machinery.

After the war public demand for motors far outstripped supply, and prices shot up. By 1923 Morgans were being manufactured under licence by Darmont in France. The Darmont Morgan was virtually identical to the British model but was fitted with a Blackburn engine. The years before the Depression were a golden period for the Morgan factory but by 1923 the boom was over.

The company survived by reducing prices and by careful planning as improvements were introduced (helped by the loyalty of the workforce, who did not strike), as well as by continuing competition successes. By the late 1920s, however, it had become clear that the demand for light cars and cyclecars, especially three-wheelers, was falling fast. The introduction of mass-produced family cars selling at £100, such as the Ford and the Austin 7, affected Morgan particularly badly.

In an attempt to counter this decline, HFS introduced several new models, but it was obvious that to survive he had to make major changes to his cars. Demand for the Morgan was diminishing. Total production in 1929 was 1002 vehicles; by 1934 it was 659, and in 1935 only 286.

HFS was a very shrewd businessman and his interpretation of the market trend in the early 1930s was brilliant. At the 1933 Motor Cycle Show he introduced the 'F' type model, which was a complete departure from his original ideas. This three-wheeler was more in line with the

Morgan three-wheelers replaced motorcycle and sidecar combinations for police patrols. Here two 1933 Family models are delivered to the Newport Police in South Wales by Alex Thom, a Newport motor agent.

design of a standard motor car and had a Ford water-cooled side-valve engine mounted in a Z-section chassis, behind an inverted V-shaped radiator. While the introduction of the 'F' type itself did very little to stem the decline in sales, it placed Morgan within one easy step of another major development if it should be necessary.

It was obvious that the motoring public was turning away from three-wheelers in vast numbers. Drastic action had to be taken. As early as 1914 HFS had experimented with a four-wheeled version of his car but had abandoned the idea. Now was the time to rethink the whole concept. The design and layout of the 'F' type were such that it was easily converted into a four-wheeler. This HFS did and, after three experimental cars had been built, the new four-wheeled Morgan (the 4-4) was announced at Christmas 1935. In keeping with his maxim that his cars must prove themselves in competition, HFS entered the final prototype in the London-Exeter Trial and timed the announcement to coincide with this. Although production of the new model did not commence until March 1936 the com-

pany produced 130 in the period to the end of December, whilst three-wheeler production was down to only 137.

In 1936 the government announced that the following year it was going to abolish the Road Fund Tax, which did away with the three-wheeler's tax advantage of only £4 per annum. Although this never happened, sales of three-wheelers declined further and by 1939 Morgan's production of them was down to only twenty-nine, whereas the production of the 4-4 model was 234 and increasing steadily. Again success in competition, particularly in the Le Mans 24 Hour Race and the RAC Rallies, played a big part in boosting orders. The 4-4 had cost little to develop and its timely introduction clearly saved the company from going the same way as all its three-wheeler competitors. The company was therefore financially buoyant when the Second World War started in 1939.

Almost as soon as war was declared, Morgan's machine shops were made over to the manufacture of essential precision parts for the Oerlikon gun and various hydraulic undercarriage components, gauges, compressor parts and such like for aircraft. There was no production of cars during this war.

When the war ended in 1945, the company was in exceptionally good financial shape, but the return to car production took much longer than after the First World War. It was eighteen months before the workforce was complete again. The cars produced in this period were mainly for export, with only a small percentage finding their way on to the home market, and these were often in chassis form, so that many strange bodies appeared on Morgan cars. By 1952 there was no demand at all for the three-wheeler and HFS reluctantly decided to end its production.

His son, Peter Morgan, was educated at Oundle and in 1936 entered the Chelsea College of Automobile Engineering; on the outbreak of war he enlisted in the Royal Army Service Corps and became a workshop officer. He was posted to Africa and ended up in charge of the Army workshop in Nairobi. After being released in 1946 with the rank of captain, he immediately joined the company as a director and as the Development Engineer/Draughtsman. When George Goodall died in 1958 Peter took over as managing director and the following year, on the death of his father, he became chairman. Therefore he had very little time to continue his highly successful competition driving. However, he did return to trials competition for a short time, driving the prototype Plus 4 Plus model.

These changes at Morgan coincided with a general slump in the world car market. If the company was to survive, there had to be an all-out effort to increase production and sales and to reduce costs. The depression was particularly acute in the United States (Morgan's main export market). This alone was almost disastrous for them and in the late 1950s and early 1960s Peter Morgan resisted a few tentative takeover offers from much larger motor manufacturers. Morgan learnt never again to be dependent on one major export market.

However, Chris Lawrence's success in the 1962 Le Mans 24 Hour Race, the resulting Plus 4 Super Sports model and the introduction of the controversial Plus 4 Plus fixed-head coupé drew the attention of the motoring press and public to the marque. While the Plus 4 Super Sports was an unqualified success, the Plus 4 Plus did not sell well but its design, revolutionary for a Morgan with its fully enclosed fibreglass body, received a lot of publicity.

As the company's finances began to recover it was decided to redistribute the capital shares, and it became a private company with Peter Morgan trading as The Morgan Motor Company. In 1970 it became a limited company again.

The development of the Plus 8 model and the acquisition of the adjoining property in the late 1960s and early 1970s was achieved without recourse to outside funding. Sales continued to increase and by 1979 the time from ordering to delivery was about five years, which still applies today.

Peter Morgan's son Charles was educated at Oundle, like his father, and then at Sussex University, and became a television cameraman, covering the trouble spots of the world. He began motor-racing in 1975 and carried on the family tradition of competition successes, driving Morgans; he was British Sports Car Champion in 1978 and 1979 in the works Plus 8. He joined the company in 1984, later becoming Production Director.

After the death of his father, Charles Morgan inherited the business. Since then he has implemented many changes throughout the factory to increase production and efficiency. The Aero 8 with its controversial styling, is his own concept. With the introduction of this model he is following in his father's footsteps, as Peter Morgan had done something similar when he introduced the Plus 4 Plus after taking over the factory when his own father, HFS, died. However, it would appear that the Aero 8 is far more successful than the Plus 4 Plus.

A Standard Runabout from 1912. Cars from that year had open tails; 1913 cars had the top part of the rear wheel enclosed. The Standard model was withdrawn in 1915 but reappeared six years later as the New Standard Popular.

MORGAN CARS

THREE-WHEELERS

Many factors govern the introduction of new models by motor manufacturers but three are fundamental: what the public think they want; what the manufacturer is able to produce; and above all the timing of the introduction.

The first factor is clearly illustrated by the change from a single-seater in 1910 to a two-seater for HFS's Standard Runabout within the space of eighteen months. Continually improved, this model remained in production until 1928. Among the improvements made in this period were an optional four-speed gearbox (normally two-speed), front-wheel brakes, electric lighting, an electric horn and a double windscreen. In 1913 a Commercial Carrier version was on offer, designed for the 'conveyance of small parcels'. The carrying space was obtained by fitting a container over the tail from the rear of the seats. This unit was hinged to give access to the rear wheel and could be removed. The model disappeared from the catalogue in 1915 but reappeared in 1921 as the New Standard Popular and continued until 1928.

In 1913 the Grand Prix model was introduced after the victory of W. G. McMinnies at the first Cyclecar Grand Prix of France at Amiens, for which three versions longer and wider than the 'Standard' model were produced. The company immediately advertised that they could supply exact copies. Versions 1 and 2 were fitted with JAP side-valve engines, with slight variations in the bodywork, for £105. Version 3 was an exact copy of the winning car and was fitted with an overhead-valve water-cooled JAP for £115. At the Motor Cycle Show that year the whole of the next year's production was ordered, including 150 for export to

Both the Sporting and the De Luxe of 1912 had more enclosed bodywork but the De Luxe had the added refinement of a door to facilitate entry and exit.

France. This was without doubt the sportiest of the Morgan range and continued until 1926, when the Aero model became more popular. Over the years it had been offered with a choice of engines: Anzani, Baker Precision, Blackburn, JAP and MAG.

In 1917 the four-seater Family model (experimented with in 1912) was announced, but it did not go on sale until the 1919 Olympia show. Fitted with an adjustable front seat, so that an adult could sit in the back, it was Morgan's answer to cheap models like the Austin 7. As improvements were made they were

The Grand Prix model was available immediately after Morgan's success in the French Cyclecar Grand Prix. These two 1913 examples were owned by the Frys of Bristol, father and son.

The four-seater prototype dated from 1912-13. HFS and Ruth share the front seats and his sister Dorothy and Ruth's brother Geoffrey Day are the rear-seat passengers.

incorporated into all models, so that they become extremely popular with the public. In 1929 the 'Carrier' body (which fitted over the rear seats from immediately behind the front seats) was reintroduced, together with a 'Delivery' van, but neither proved popular and very few were sold. In 1931 a redesigned body was fitted almost exclusively to the Family De Luxe model and was produced alongside bodies of the original shape. In the same year the 'Sports Family Model' was introduced. Built on a 'C' type chassis, it had De Luxe specifications, a boat-tailed four-seater body and exposed engine, and

it remained in production until 1936.

The 'Aero' model was announced at the 1920 Olympia Motor Cycle Show. Fitted with two half-round wind deflectors, named 'Aero-screens', the model was exceedingly popular, and a sportier version, the 'Super Sports Aero', was offered from 1928. The model stayed in production until 1933 and underwent many mechanical and body changes, notably the introduction of the 'M' type chassis, with underslung rear suspension, in 1929. This enabled the rear wheel to be easily removed. An 'Aero Family' model was also available. Further changes were

A 1926 Aero with water-cooled side-valve JAP engine and Ghost silencers. Note the youthful driver: the Morgan three-wheeler was classed as a motorcycle and in 1926 it was legal for a fourteen-year-old to ride a motorcycle.

This specially bodied Super Sports of 1933 shows the horizontal spare-wheel mounting and the exhaust pipes lowered 6 inches (152 mm) in an effort to prevent passengers burning their sleeves and elbows.

made to the chassis design so that a three-speed gearbox could be used, with a new 1096 cc JAP air- or water-cooled engine in side- or overhead-valve versions. Slowly the Aero was phased out and in 1932 the new 'Super Sports' became the model available. At the same time the 'Sports' model was also announced; it was fitted with a Matchless MX or MX2 engine, and later with the MX4. Produc-

tion of all these models continued until 1939.

The 'F' type Ford-engined model, introduced at the 1933 Olympia Motor Cycle Show, was a complete departure from all previous Morgans, except that it still had three wheels. Fitted with an in-line four-cylinder Ford engine which was mounted into a Z-section chassis, as opposed to the Morgan tubular chassis, the

The problem of where to mount the spare wheel was finally solved in 1935 with the modification of the rear bodywork of the Super Sports to create the 'barrelback'.

Morgan versatility: this 1934 JAP-engined Super Sports was well able to cope with another two wheels and the weight of boat and trailer.

'F' four-seater Morgan was known as the 'F4'; the two-seater introduced in 1935 was the 'F2'. In 1937 there appeared the 'F Super Sports' ('F Super'), which combined the front half of the F2 with the rear half of the V-twin Super Sports. This variation was easily recognisable from the front by the additional line of louvres along the tops of both halves of the bonnet and the cycle-type front wings. Although production of the 'F' types recommenced after the war, by 1952 production of all three-wheeler models was ended.

A post-war F Super used the E93A Ford engine from the Ford 10. Production continued until 1952.

The experimental four-wheeled Morgan (1935) was based on an 'F' type three-wheeler chassis. The chassis side members were aligned, a conventional rear axle fitted, and the mobile test bed was created.

FOUR-WHEELERS

The design of the 'F' type was the perfect test bed for an experimental four-wheeled Morgan. By fitting a conventional rear axle, straightening the chassis sides and adding the extra wheel, it was achieved with the minimum of extra work. However, it soon became obvious that the Ford engine was not powerful enough and it was replaced by the 1122 cc Coventry Climax overhead-inlet and side-exhaust valve engine, which had proved to be so reliable in such cars as the Crossley Regis and Triumph Gloria.

In order to prove his new 4-4 (four wheels, four cylinders) in competition, HFS timed the announcement of the model in December 1935 to coincide with his entry in the London-Exeter Trial, just as he had done with his first three-wheeler. The car performed well, gaining a Premier Award and special mention in the

A works 4-4 two-seater that was used in several competitions c.1938, here photographed at Madresfield Court, Worcestershire, with a friend of the works manager, George Goodall, at the wheel.

15

Production of the four-seater 4-4 started at the end of 1937. The wheelbase was the same as that of the two-seater; the rear seat was made possible by taking space from the luggage area and repositioning the fuel tank and battery.

motoring press for its hill-climbing ability. Once again sales figures reflected competition success and by 1937 demand was comfortably outstripping production capacity. This demand led Morgan to introduce the four-seater and drop-head coupé variants. Then, after success in the 1938 Le Mans 24 Hour Race, a more sporting version using the 1098 cc Coventry Climax competition engine was announced, but only a few were produced before war was declared.

As production slowly returned to normal after the war the 4-4 was powered by a 1267 cc Standard Special engine, a few of which had been experimented with before the war, because Coventry Climax stopped production of the previous engines. Whether by design or by slip of the pen, the name also changed immediately after the war, from 4-4 to 4/4. Production ended in 1951 with the introduction of the Plus 4. This model, in its various guises, was to become the flagship of the company and opened an era in which Morgan again excelled in motor sport throughout the world.

In this new model the Standard 1267 cc unit was replaced by a 2088 cc four-cylinder overhead-valve Standard Vanguard engine, which was the best Morgan could find. As it replaced the 4/4, the new model was produced in all the same variants as its predecessor, its body dimensions being only slightly larger. One major innovation was the semi-automatic lubrication of the sliding sleeves of the swivels of the front suspension, actuated

The introduction of the 'Interim Radiator' Plus 4 was forced on the company by diminishing supplies of integral radiators and freestanding headlamps. This is a 'high lamp' version, required to meet the new lighting regulations introduced in the United Kingdom in 1954.

This Vanguard-engined drop-head coupé was originally built as a flat-radiator model and left the works in August 1954. Having languished with the main agents for a year, it was returned to the works, rebodied with a cowled radiator and resold to another agent, leaving the factory in October 1955. Several flat-radiator cars were remodelled in this way.

by the driver via a foot-operated valve in the cockpit. It was produced until 1954, when parts manufacturers were phasing out production of free-standing headlamps and integral radiators as cars became streamlined. Morgan decided to change the body shape rather than make their own parts, which would have been expensive.

The transition to the fully enclosed radiator and headlamps came in two stages. First the headlamps were enclosed in the wings, and the pressurised radiator behind a flat sloping grille. Only a few of this model were produced. Then the grille was changed to the now familiar curved profile. Later changes included replacement of the twin upright spare wheels by a single wheel inserted into the sloping rear panel.

In 1953 the Vanguard engine was phased out, to be replaced by the Triumph TR2 engine. Priced at about £830, the Plus 4 was the cheapest British car capable of reaching 100 mph (160 km/h). The model continued, using in turn the TR3, TR4 and TR4A engines as they became available from Triumph.

The Plus 4 Super Sports model came about as a result of Chris Lawrence's remarkable achievement at the 1962 Le Mans 24 Hour Race. As in 1913, a model based on the successful race car was soon available to the public. With Peter Morgan, Chris Lawrence had worked on the development of the race car and had done most of the tuning. Under an agreement with the company all engines used

The Plus 4 Super Sports model used Triumph TR4 or TR4A engines, which were sent to Lawrence Tune at Westerham Motors, Acton, in west London. There they were stripped down, all internal moving parts were balanced, the cylinder head was polished and gas-flowed and modified inlet manifold Weber carburettors were fitted.

Although the design was not well accepted by the motoring public when it was introduced, the Plus 4 Plus is now a highly sought-after collector's car This rear quarter view clearly shows the influence of the contemporary Lotus on the design.

in the new model were sent to him to receive the 'Lawrence Tune' treatment, which comprised expert tuning and balancing, different carburettors, inlet and exhaust manifolds. The engines were then returned to the factory and fitted into a light-alloy body. A total of 104 of this model were produced and they proved to be the salvation of the company.

In 1965 the company produced a cheaper version of the Super Sports, named the 'Plus 4 Competition' model, in which the engine did not receive the full Lawrence Tune treatment but did include the manifolds.

The standard Morgan chassis required few alterations to achieve the fitting of the new-style body, revolutionary for Morgan, of the Plus 4 Plus fixed-head coupé. Although it proved its capabilities

in competition in the hands of Peter Morgan, the model did not attract sales. In all only twenty-six were produced, spread over just under three years.

In 1955 the factory reintroduced the 4/4 model, powered by a Ford 10 horsepower engine, to fill a gap in the market for a cheap sports car. It was popular and has continued in production ever since, with new Ford engines as they became available. Fitting a new engine necessitated certain changes to the chassis and bodywork, but the basic body shape, suspension and chassis design have remained, apart from improvements to keep pace with motoring technology. The Ford engine has been replaced by the Duratec V6 engine.

Production of all Plus 4s ended in January 1969 when Triumph announced that they

The prototype Plus 8 had two bulges in the bonnet to allow room to fit the dashpots of the two SU carburettors. Note the wire-spoked wheels; only three Plus 8s were fitted with this type of wheel. Before it went into production a completely new wheel design was necessary to handle the torque generated by the V8 engine.

New Morgans, lined up in the finishing and distribution bay at the works, await collection by their owners in 1993.

were no longer producing the four-cylinder TR engines. Morgans then relied entirely on the Ford-engined 4/4 until the Plus 8 model was introduced at the end of that year, whereupon the production of both models ran side by side.

In 1966 a director of Rover Cars who was visiting the Morgan factory asked how Morgan would receive a takeover offer from Rover. Politely declining any offer about to be made, Peter Morgan seized the opportunity and tentatively suggested that he would be interested in using the new Buick (General Motors) V8 3.5 litre engine, of which Rover had just acquired the rights in the United Kingdom. To his amazement the Rover director agreed in principle. The subsequent supply of experimental engines and agreement from General Motors that the engine could be used by Morgan did not come easily. Eventually all the necessary permissions were obtained and development of the new model, the Plus 8, continued apace. The whole development was carried out by Maurice Owen, Morgan's Development Engineer. The new model was announced in October 1968 at the Earl's Court Motor Show and was an instant success with both the motoring press and the public. Like all Morgan models, the Plus 8 continued to be developed, until it was replaced in 2004 by the 'Roadster' model. This outwardly

The works prototype fuel-injected Plus 8.

No mass-production techniques are used in the Morgan factory. Here Plus 8 chassis are mounted on trestles, with engines, rear axles and components laid out ready for assembly. The chassis on the right has a galvanised finish, offered as an option by the Morgan works. This scene represents a week's production of ten to twelve cars.

This publicity photograph, issued for the launch of the Rover-engined Plus 4 in 1988, was staged in the factory yard with the aid of one or two props. The stained glass window above the door was presented to Peter Morgan by the Plus 4 Club of California to mark the seventy-fifth anniversary of the company in 1984.

resembles a Plus 8, but the new model is fitted with a Ford 3 litre V6 engine. Despite being a similar capacity, this engine develops more power: 217 bhp, as opposed to the 190 bhp of the Rover engine. The car is therefore lighter and faster.

In 1985 Morgan introduced another Plus 4 model. This one was offered with a Fiat 2 litre engine which the company decided would fit nicely between the basic 4/4 and the high-performance Plus 8 models. The new model was designated by the factory as a Plus 4 but was never 'type approved', and therefore a 'certificate of newness' from the factory could not carry the Plus 4 designation, although the Plus 4 badge was fitted to the cars. Production ended in January 1987. However, when Rover introduced the M16 'lean burn' sixteen-valve fuel-injected 2 litre engine, Morgan switched to this power unit. The model, launched in May 1988, is still in production, using the more advanced Rover T16 engine. This time the designation 'Plus 4' was 'type approved'.

The very first competition appearance of a Morgan: HFS driving his single-seater with tiller steering in the first London-Exeter Trial, Boxing Day 1910.

MORGANS IN COMPETITION

THREE-WHEELERS

The main reason for the continued existence of the Morgan Motor Company, the oldest motor manufacturer in the world that is still a family firm, is its outstanding successes in competition down the years.

In an International Scratch Race organised by the British Motor Cycle Racing Club at Brooklands in 1912 a two-seater Morgan was entered, driven by Harry Martin and carrying a passenger. Martin took the lead from the start, completing the first lap at 53 mph (85 km/h), and the second at just under 60 mph (96 km/h). Such was his speed that he finished over two minutes ahead of the second-placed Sebella-JAP. As a result the Brooklands officials decided that all future cyclecar races were to be handicapped. Within a week of the race HFS received over a hundred orders, and he was forced to expand his works to increase his output to twenty cars per week.

In order to stimulate the cyclecar in-

dustry, a new motoring magazine called *Cyclecar* was introduced in 1912 and *Motor Cycling* magazine donated a trophy which was to be awarded at the end of each year to the holder of the cyclecar one-hour record. Competition between manufacturers was intense and it became evident that the two main contestants were Morgan and GWK, a two-cylinder friction-drive four-wheeler. On 9th November HFS easily won the One Hour Race at Brooklands, beating J. Wood's GWK, which had suffered from water in the electrical system. He had also beaten Wood's records, one for the distance covered in one hour, and the other for the time taken to cover 50 miles (80.5 km). A few days later Wood returned to Brooklands and retook both records. The reputation of the Morgan was at stake, as were its sales, and HFS returned to Brooklands on 23rd November and added over 3 miles (4.8 km) to Wood's distance and reduced the 50 mile record to 50 minutes 28.6 seconds. No further attempts were made on

Above: *HFS at the start of the ACU Six Day Trial, August 1913. He won a gold award.*

Right: *Lieutenant R. T. Messeroy and HFS nearing the summit of the 1 in 3 Old Wyche cutting in the Birmingham Trial, 1914.*

Left: *Freddie James takes to the water in the 1920 Six Day Trial.*

the records before the end of the year, so Morgan won the Cyclecar Trophy.

Morgans continued to triumph, not only in Britain, but on the continent as well, in events entered by both private and works drivers. Morgan's chief rivals were the many light cars and cyclecars produced in the 1920s by companies as eager as Morgan for competition success not only in track racing, but in economy trials, reliability trails, hill-climbs and all types of motor sport. However, the Morgan Runabout presented the organisers of such events with the problem of how to classify the vehicle. It was obviously not a motorcycle combination, although many thought it should be, but was it a car? Eventually it was classed as a cyclecar by the British Automobile Racing Club and the Royal Automobile Club Competition Department. This caused problems for the manufacturers of four-wheelers because the Morgan's amazing power to weight ratio, its tractability and reliability, together with the increasing number of good drivers using the car in competition, led to almost total domination in motor sport

at that level. The Morgan was an embarrassment to all organisers and in particular the Junior Car Club, which in conjunction with the BARC organised most of the racing for light cars and cyclecars at the Brooklands race track. They were always looking for a way of banning Morgans from the races so that other vehicles could appear in the results, and severe handicaps were allocated to Morgans in order to reduce their success rate.

In the JCC's International 200 Mile Light Car Race in September 1924, a works Morgan driven by E. B. Ware, with a riding mechanic named Allchin, was travelling at over 85 mph (137 km/h) on the thirty-third lap when the rear wheel started to wobble, and two laps later the car suddenly swerved, hit the fence and spun round on the track. Ware and Allchin were thrown out of the car. Both survived but Ware never raced again. With the backing of the BARC the JCC banned all three-wheeler cars from competing in long-distance races and high-speed trials. However, Morgan continued to compete

E. B. Ware after his victory in the Light-car Long Handicap Race at Brooklands, May 1920.

Freddie James, seen here on Ilkley Moor, won a silver medal with his Family Aero in the 1928 International Six Day Trial.

in rallies and trials, and to break world records. In 1928, after much negotiation between the Morgan Motor Company and the BARC, a new club was formed, the Cyclecar Club, which was allowed to organise and race at Brooklands. Morgans were back in racing again.

Of the numerous types of competition held at that time, Morgan excelled at trials, which were held over a period ranging from one to six days. The most famous trials were those organised by the Motor Cycling Club (MCC): the London-Exeter, the London-Edinburgh and the London-Land's End. As well as 'on road' timings between checkpoints, these events included special speed sections and hill-climbs run over scree, parts of which could be steeper than 1 in 3.

Racing at Brooklands at speeds between 80 and 90 mph (130-145 km/h) inevitably led to the breaking of lap speed and distance speed records. For example, at the JCC Spring Meeting in 1922 E. B. Ware broke the flying 5 miles (8 km) and the standing mile records with speeds of 83.26 mph (134 km/h) and 79.60 mph (128 km/h) respectively. Many of the great names in Morgan competition success were actively engaged in record attempts but, as there was a prize and sponsorship money available for each new record set, records were broken only by a few miles per hour at a time, although on many occasions

The Morgan team at Brooklands during the 1921 ACU Six Day Trial: HFS and Mrs Morgan (90), Frank Boddington (91) and Billy Elces (92).

drivers and vehicles were capable of much faster speeds on the day. Douglas Hawkes, for example, a prolific record setter, was sponsored by Shell, Castrol, KLG Plugs, CAC Coil Ignition, Coventry Chains, Solex Carburettors and Dunlop Tyres.

Record setting was not just a male preserve. One of the most prolific drivers was Gwenda Stewart, who on 7th September 1929 achieved the incredible feat of covering 101.55 miles (163.4 km) in an hour. This was the first time that a three-wheeler had ever covered the magic 100 miles (161 km) in an hour; the motorcycle combination record at that time stood at 89.4 miles (143.9 km). To mark this outstanding achievement, she was entertained to luncheon by HFS at Malvern and was presented with a gold chronograph which had been subscribed to by Morgan and the manufacturers of the various components used on her car. In May 1930 she set a new twenty-four-hour record in twenty-one hours and therefore stopped, as all she would have achieved by continuing would have been an extension of the distance. In June she achieved

113.52 mph (182.7 km/h) for 5 kilometres, and 107.51 mph (173.0 km/h) for 5 miles. In August she achieved an amazing 115.66 mph (186.1 km/h) for the flying kilometre. In all she established a total of fifty-seven records in the year.

FOUR-WHEELERS

Success in all types of competition did not slacken with the introduction of the four-wheeled Morgan in 1936. The first race for the 4-4 was the Ulster Trophy in June 1937, which was won by Robert Campbell, a Belfast mechanic. In July the Leinster Trophy Race was won by D. C. McCracken. In the RAC Rally works driver George Goodall won the Group 1 prize.

1938 was a highly successful year for Morgans. In the RAC Rally George Goodall won the Group 1 prize and all the other Morgans entered won prizes in their respective classes. In the Le Mans 24 Hour Race, a first-time entrant, Miss Prudence Fawcett, with her co-driver Geoffrey White, finished second in their class and thirteenth overall, covering 1372.98 miles (2209.5 km) at an average of 57.2 mph

'Uncle' George Goodall, the works manager, and his son, 'Sonny' Jim Goodall, competing in the 1938 RAC Rally in one of the 1122 cc 4-4s, which had been modified to cycle-type front wings. They finished first in class and took a Premier Award.

Prudence Fawcett and Geoffrey White during practice in the 1938 Le Mans 24 Hour race. This was Miss Fawcett's first and only international race.

(92 km/h), qualifying for the Rudge-Whitworth Biennial Cup. In the MCC Trials Peter Morgan won a coveted Gold Medal Triple Award given to any driver who succeeded in gaining a Premier Award in all three trials in one year. Only two were awarded that year, the other going to H. F. S. Morgan.

The following year was again dominated by Morgan successes in two major events. George Goodall won Group 1 of the RAC Rally for the third year in succession, beating forty-one other entries in that group. At Le Mans Dick Anthony and Geoffrey White finished fifteenth overall, having covered 1548.62 miles (2492.2 km) at an average of 64.53 mph (103.9 km/h).

Competition events, cancelled for the duration of the war, began to return to normal in 1949 and before long Morgan regained dominance in their group in all major rallies.

Henry Laird makes a pit stop during practice in the 1938 Tourist Trophy race at Donnington.

Journalists Peter Garnier of 'Autocar' and Charles Heywood compete in Peter Morgan's personal Plus 4 drop-head coupé in the 1954 Exeter Trial. They gained a Silver Award.

In the 1951 RAC International Rally of Great Britain Morgan very nearly beat the Jaguar works team, with all its huge financial backing. Of the 267 entries thirty-seven were Jaguar XK120s. However, Morgan was able to win the coveted team award from them, by 2.15 marks, and they won it again in 1952.

The difficulties for the company brought about by the depression in the United States were eased by increased sales following the success of Chris Lawrence in the 1962 Le Mans 24 Hour Race. Chris Lawrence and Richard Shepherd-Baron drove an uneventful race until 7 a.m. on Sunday, when an exhaust pipe broke close to the manifold. An attempt was made to secure it but rather than waste time the car rejoined the race sounding like a Grand Prix car. In spite of this they continued to lap at close on 100 mph (160 km/h). Fifty-five cars started the race and only eighteen finished, with the Morgan finishing thirteenth overall. More important, they had won the 2 litre class at an average speed of 93.97 mph (151.2 km/h), having covered 2255 miles (3629 km) in the twenty-four hours.

In Chris Lawrence's first full season of racing in 1959 he won nine marque races and a handicap race. He also came second four times and third once and finished in every race. Here he leads the field in the BRSCC Brands Hatch marque race on 10th May, when he achieved his first win in a Morgan.

Left: *In 1961 Pip Arnold competed in the Coppa Inter-Europa race at Monza in XRX 1, which was fitted with an experimental hardtop that was eventually marketed to Morgan owners.*

Right: *Peter Morgan, with Mrs Jane Morgan in the passenger seat, strives to maintain adhesion and motion in his 4/4 in the MMEC/ Shenstone/Morgan Clubs' Production Trial in March 1963.*

Left: *Dixon Smith in the prototype Series II 4/4, competing in the Curborough Sprint meeting.*

Right: *Dixon Smith also competed very success-fully in his four-seater Plus 4 drop-head coupé. It is seen here accelerat-ing hard in an inter-club hill-climb at Shelsley Walsh in July 1964.*

On the east coast of the United States one of the best-known and most successful Morgan owners and competitors is John H. Sheally II. His collection of Morgans is known worldwide. Here he is seen taking the chequered flag in his modified Cosworth-engined 4/4 on winning the class 'D' Modified Sports Car race at Southside Speedway, Richmond, Virginia, in July 1987.

In another highly modified 4/4, Peter Askew competes in the Bentley Drivers' Club Morgans Only Race at Silverstone in 1988. His car was the highest placed 4/4, behind the big-engined Plus 8s.

In 1962, in response to public objections to night driving at high speeds and other disturbances caused by rallies, government legislation all but ended road rallying in Britain. It was one of the most popular types of motor sport amongst private owners so it was not long before they found other forms of competition. Morgan was more than up to the challenge, most notably in marque racing, sprints and hillclimbs, especially with the Plus 4 Super Sports model, which was developed as a result of the Le Mans race.

The Plus 4 model was succeeded in 1969 by the Plus 8, powered by the 3.5 litre Rover engine, and it was not long before the new model was competing suc-

cessfully. Ford-powered models, too, continued to win events, but their successes were mostly confined to class wins and records rather than overall wins.

This chapter has presented just a brief outline of Morgan's remarkable history of success in competition over the years. Readers who seek more detail should consult some of the other books listed under 'Further Reading'. Morgan and Morgan owners still compete in all manner of events around the world and without doubt will continue to do so for years to come. There is no other marque which can even begin to match the consistency of the Morgan. The Morgan car is in a class of its own in the history of motoring.

LIST OF MODELS PRODUCED

This list includes all Morgan models with their dates of production.

THREE-WHEELERS
Standard, 1910-28
Grand Prix, 1913-26
Family four-seater, 1917-37
Sports Family, 1931-6
Family De Luxe, 1930-2
'Delivery' van, 1933-5
Aero prototypes, 1916-20
Aero, 1920-33
Aero Family, 1926-33
Super Sports Aero, 1927-33
Super Sports, 1932-7
Sports, 1932-9
Ford-engined models:
  F2, F4 and F Super, 1933-52

FOUR-WHEELERS
4-4 and 4/4, 1936-51
4-4 Le Mans Replica and Tourist Trophy Replica,
  1939
4/4 Series II, 1955-60
4/4 Series III, 1960-1
4/4 Series IV, 1961-3
4/4 Series V, 1963-8
4/4 Ford 1600, 1968-71
4/4 Ford GT 1600, 1968-82
4/4 Fiat 1600, 1981-5
4/4 1600 CHV, 1982-91

4/4 Ford 1800, 1993 continuing
4/4 Ford 1600 EFI, 1991-3
4/4 1600cc Ford engine, 2004 continuing
Aero 8 4398cc BMW engine, 2004 continuing
Plus 4 Vanguard engine, 1951-4
Plus 4 Interim and cowled radiator, 1953-8
Plus 4 Drop-head coupé, 1951-6
Plus 4 Triumph TR2 engine, 1954-8
Plus 4 Triumph TR3 engine, 1956-64
Plus 4 Triumph TR4 and TR4A engines, 1962-9
Plus 4 Super Sports, 1961-8
Plus 4 Competition, 1965-7
Plus 4 Plus, 1964-7
SLR, 1963-4
Plus 4 Fiat engine, 1985-7
Plus 4 Rover M16 engine, 1989-92
Plus 4 Rover T16 engine, 1992 continuing
Plus 4 1994cc Rover t16 engine, 1992-2000
Plus 4 2 litre Duratec engine, 2000 continuing
Plus 4 Four seater, either 3 litre Ford or 2 litre
  Duratec engine, 2004 continuing
Plus 8, 1968 continuing
Plus 8 Sports Lightweight, 1975-7
Plus 8 3946cc engine, 1990-2004
Plus 8 4.6 litre engine, 1997-2004, replaced by
  the Roadster
Roadster 3 litre Duratec V6 engine, 2004 con-
  tinuing

FURTHER READING

THREE-WHEELERS
ABC of the Morgan. Morgan Three-wheeler Club, *c.*1960s.
Alderson, Dr J.D., and Rushton, D.M. *Morgan Sweeps the Board.* Gentry Books, 1978.
The Best of Clarrie. Morgan Three-wheeler Club, 1994.
Boddy, W. *The Vintage Years of the Morgan Three-wheeler.* Grenville Publishing, 1970.
Clarke, R.M. *The Book of the Morgan Three-wheeler.* Pitman, *c.*1960s.
Clarke, R.M. *Morgan Three-wheelers 1930-1952.* Brooklands Books, *c.*1973.
Clarke, R.M. *Morgan Three-wheeler Gold Portfolio 1910-1962.* Distributed by Brooklands Book Dis-
  tribution, 1989.
Clew, Jeff. *JAP: The Vintage Years.* Haynes, 1985.
Clew, Jeff. *JAP: The End of an Era.* Haynes, 1988.
Coombes, Clarrie. *No More Twins.* Morgan Three-wheeler Club, *c.*1965.
Davidson, Barry. *The Best of 'The Bulletin'.* Morgan Three-wheeler Club, 1973. By the editor of the
  magazine.
Hill, Ken. *Completely Morgan 1909-1952.* Veloce Publishing, 1995.
Hill, Ken. *Three-wheelers.* Shire, second edition 1995.
Jelly, Harold. *The Book of the Morgan.* Pitman, 1933 (second edition 1934, third edition 1935).
Miller, P. *Morgan Three-wheelers – The Complete Story.* Crowood Press, 2004.
Morgan, History of a Famous Car. Morgan Motor Company, new edition 1994.
Walton, G.T. *The Book of the Morgan.* Pitman, 1932.
Watts, Brian. *The Three-wheeler.* Morgan Three-wheeler Club, 1970.

FOUR-WHEELERS
Alderson, J. *Morgan Sports Cars – The Early Years.* Sheffield Academic, 1997.
Boddy, W. 'Morgan: On Four Wheels', *The Great Cars* 71 (1976), pages 1409-19.

Bowden, Gregory Houston. *More Morgan*. Gentry Books, 1976.
Bowden, Gregory Houston. *Morgan: First and Last of the Real Sports Cars*. Gentry Books, second edition 1986.
Clarke, E. *Morgan 1968–2001. A Brooklands Portfolio*. Brooklands Books, *c*.2002.
Clarke, R. *Morgan Autobook One*. Auto Press, 1968.
Clarke, R.M. (editor). *Morgan Cars 1936-1960*. Brooklands Books, *c*.1962.
Clarke, R.M. (editor). *Morgan Cars 1960-1970*. Brooklands Books, *c*.1971.
Clarke, R.M. (editor). *Morgan Cars 1969-1970*. Brooklands Books, *c*.1980.
Clarke, R.M. *Morgan Four Owners' Workshop Manual*. Distributed by Brooklands Book Distribution, *c*.1989.
Clarke, R.M. *Morgan Cars Gold Portfolio 1968-1989*. Distributed by Brooklands Book Distribution, 1989.
Clarke, R.M. *Morgan Plus 4 and Four 4 Gold Portfolio 1936-1967*. Distributed by Brooklands Book Distribution, 1993.
Dowse, D. *Morgan at Le Mans*. Tempus, 2005.
Dowdeswell, John. *The Morgan Four-wheeler Workshop Manual*. Published by the author, *c*.1960s.
Dymock, Eric. *The Plus Four Morgan*. Profile Publications, 1967.
Harvey, Chris. *Morgan, The Last Survivor*. Oxford Illustrated Press, 1987.
Hill, Ken. *The Four-Wheeled Morgan*: volume 1, 'The Flat Radiator Models'; volume 2, 'The Cowled Radiator Models'. Motor Racing Publications, 1977 and 1980.
Hill, Ken. *Completely Morgan 1936-1968*. Veloce Publishing, 1994.
Hill, Ken. *Completely Morgan from 1968*. Veloce Publishing, 1994.
Holm, Bengt Ason. *Morgan* (Famous Car Factory series). Motorbooks International, Wisconsin, USA, 1992.
Laban, B. *Morgan, The First and Last of the Real Sports Cars*. Virgin, 2000.
McComb, F. Wilson. 'Morgan', *Auto Histoire* 38. EAP, Paris, 1985.
Morgan 1910-1980. Combined Morgan Clubs, 1980.
Morgan, Buying and Restoration Book. Practical Classics & Car Restorer Magazine, 1992.
Morgan Four Owner's Workshop Manual and Buying Portfolio. Brooklands Books, *c*.2002.
Morgan Sports; From Three Wheels to Four. IPC Transport Press, 1977.
Musgrove, Colin. *Moggie: The Purchase, Maintenance and Enjoyment of Morgan Sports Cars*. Quills Publishing, 1980.
Musgrove, Colin. *The Morgan Year Book, 1980-81*. Magpie Publishing, Hong Kong, 1981.
Pearson, M. *Me, My Morgan and The Midlands*. Wayzgoose, 2002.
Price, R. *TOK258 – Morgan Winner at Le Mans*. MX Publishing, 2005.
Quirk, Terry. *The Morgan Cartoon Book*. Quills Publishing, 1980.
Rassusen, Henry, and Blakemore, John. *Postwar MGs and Morgans*. Picturama Publishing, California, 1979.
Robson, Graham. *Morgan, Plus 8*. Osprey, 1984.
Schrader, Halwart. *Morgan Sport- und Tourenwagen 1935-1981*. Schrader (S) Verlag, Germany, 1991.
Sheally, John H. *Morgans in the Colonies*. Jordan & Co, Virginia Beach, 1978.
Sheally, John H. *Morgans, Pride of the British*. TAB Books Inc, Pennsylvania, USA, 1982.
Sheally II, J.H. *The Rare Ones. Peter Morgan and the Plus 4 Plus*. Rank & File Publications, 2002.
Teague, John. *Plus 4 Super Profile*. Haynes, 1987.
Tipler, John. *Morgan: The Cars and the Factory*. Crowood Press, 1993.
Worrall, J. *Original Morgan – 4/4, Plus 4, and Plus 8*. Bay View Books, 1992.

THREE- AND FOUR-WHEELERS
Bell, R. *Morgans to 1997 – A Collector's Guide*. Motor Racing Publications, 1997.
Hill, Ken. *Morgan 75 Years on the Road*. Blandford Press, 1984.
Hill, Ken. *Illustrated Morgan Buyers' Guide*. Motorbooks International, Wisconsin, USA, second edition 1990.
Hill, Ken. *Morgan – The Best of British in Old Photographs*. Allan Sutton Publishing Ltd, 1997.
Hill, Ken. *The Art of Selling a Unique Sports Car*. Blandford Press, 1996.
Isaac, R. *Morgan – Osprey Classic Marques*. Osprey, 1994.
Wood, J. *Morgan Performance Plus Tradition*. Haynes, 2004.

PLACES TO VISIT

These museums are known normally to have Morgans on exhibition. Visitors should check the times and dates of opening before travelling. Other museums which are not listed may have Morgans on display.

C. M. Booth Collection of Historic Vehicles, 63 High Street, Rolvenden, Cranbrook, Kent TN17
    4LP. Telephone: 01580 241234. Website: www.morganmuseum.org.uk A unique collection of
    Morgan three-wheelers.
Heritage Motor Centre, Banbury Road, Gaydon, Warwick CV35 0BJ.
    Telephone: 01926 641188. Website: www.heritage-motor-centre.co.uk
Lakeland Motor Museum, Holker Hall and Gardens, Cark-in-Cartmel, Grange-over-Sands, South
    Lakeland, Cumbria LA11 7PL. Telephone: 01539 530400.
    Website: www.lakelandmotormuseum.co.uk
Llangollen Motor Museum, Pentre Felin, Llangollen, North Wales LL20 8EE.
    Telephone: 01978 860324. Website: www.llangollenmotormuseum.co.uk
Morgan Motor Company Ltd, Pickersleigh Road, Malvern Link, Worcestershire WR14 2LL.
    Telephone: 01684 573104. Website www.morgan-motor.co.uk
National Motor Museum, John Montagu Building, Beaulieu, Brockenhurst, Hampshire SO42 7ZN.
    Telephone: 01590 614650. Website: www.nationalmotormuseum.org.uk
Science Museum, Exhibition Road, South Kensington, London SW7 2DD.
    Telephone: 0870 870 4868. Website: www.sciencemuseum.org.uk

CLUBS
    There are clubs for Morgan owners and enthusiasts throughout the world. They include:
The Morgan Sports Car Club Ltd. Membership Secretary: Mrs Anne Salisbury, 7 Woodland Grove,
    Dudley, West Midlands DY3 2XB. Telephone: 01384 254480. Website: www.mscc.uk.com
The Morgan Three-Wheeler Club Ltd. Membership Secretary: Maria Parkinson, 26 Hamilton Road,
    Taunton, Somerset TA1 2ER. Website: www.mtwc.co.uk

Morgan enthusiast Cyril Charlesworth tackles Tillerton in the 1964 MCC Exeter Trial.